THE CANADIAN BRASS

Book of easy quintets
With discussion and techniques

By WALTER H. BARNES

Contents

E   Easy   M   Medium   D   Difficult

A 'note' to you (T.B.T.)

Ensemble playing is one of the great rewards of Instrumental Music. YOU ARE IMPORTANT!!! You cannot be 'covered', or your sound hidden. You stand on your own, with your musical friends needing you as you need them. As you progress through our book, you become a better listener as well as a better performer. All your other musical groups (bands, orchestras) benefit from your experience here. But, most of all, this ensemble book introduces you to a new world of musical enjoyment and equal participation.

We want to stress three basics: **Tone, Balance, and Tuning**

Music is different from all other Art forms in that sound is more important than what is seen. Your *Tone* should be free-flowing, sitting on the air column with ease, round, well-focused, and able to blend with your ensemble. You must always listen to yourself and concern yourself with the best sound that you can make.

Now, bring your tone to your ensemble and realize that the political phrase of Equality has never been truer. You must be an equal part of your small group, not more – not less. *Balance* your sound by listening to the others. At times you will have the melody or the projecting part; your friends will support you. Other times will require that you support your partners. This is done by listening and balancing your part in an equal but changeable relation to the whole sound.

Equality has its foundation in relationship to others. So does *Tuning*. You must listen all around you, but especially to your foundation – the Tuba or the lowest instrument playing at the time. If you are the Tuba player, you must be very careful to place each note in tune so that you provide a consistent foundation for the others. Before you begin performing, tune your instruments together on a concert B^b. Then, play the last note of the piece and fit into the chord. Your note will have a proper place that helps the chord shine. The secret is – careful listening in a musical relationship with your friends. We suggest that you acquire from your music store, the cassette tape (recorded by us) of the music in this book.

Most of the selections that we have arranged here were purposely chosen from Choral literature! But take heart and heed, fellow Brass players. Choral music is the marriage of word and note phrases making music sentences and, collectively, sound paragraphs. Inherent in a successful presentation is the punctuation – breathing marks. We have carefully marked each selection so that you are better able to 'sing' each phrase, supporting your sound with an intensity of air column for your tonal production. Follow these breathmarks (') as an indication of phrases.

We have only marked the basic dynamics. We hope that you (with the entire group), after learning the notes and phrases, will develop *your own* interpretation, and therefore your own volume markings. (We have provided 'tempo' suggestions.) Your creativity, rather than the imposition of our interpretation, will enable your ensemble to grow together musically.

Have fun!

Canadian Brass

THE CANADIAN BRASS

Book of easy quintets
With discussion and techniques

By WALTER H. BARNES

Arranged for:
1st (B♭) Trumpet
2nd (B♭) Trumpet
Horn in F
→ Trombone
Tuba
Conductor

DISTRIBUTED BY

HAL•LEONARD®
CORPORATION
7777 W. BLUEMOUND RD. P.O. BOX 13819 MILWAUKEE, WI 53213

THE CANADIAN BRASS EDUCATIONAL SERIES

Warm-up

Editor Gentlemen. Could we have a discussion on the very important area of warm-up. I see so many students who literally 'grab' their instrument out of their case and begin playing. What do *you* do?

Tuba The first thing I do is play a long single note on the mouthpiece. That's to loosen up the lips and find pitch through the middle of the air column. Then, try a very simple four-note mouthpiece warm-up for a minute or two (notes: f g a g f e f). Then, play a scale – again on the mouthpiece – making pitches really in tune with each other.

Trombone Basically the same thing for the Trombone. I would try to start with the pitch. I think that pitch is so very important so you know what pitch is in your head and relate it to the embouchure. Remember, when you're warming up, you're working on not only your lip and face muscles, but the breathing muscles (rib cage and diaphragm). Take a lot of air in, blowing air through the mouthpiece. 4th line 'f' is a good note to start on. (Use your Trombone to find that f, then work on the mouthpiece only.) You can also play any melody you like. Then start to relate your pitches to the instrument, usually just long tones, similar to what the scales are.

Horn The horn player first of all finds the horn pitch and then uses the mouthpiece to do patterns, breathing as often as necessary, using lots of air. Then go to the horn after the lip feels it's responding and play a pattern such as this: c d c e c f c g c a c b c c c; *then*: c g c e g e c g c e g e g e c. When the student becomes more familiar with the horn, use all the various fingerings starting with an open F horn, second valve, first valve, first and second together, second and third together in those same patterns. Horn players must make sure that their hand does not close off the bell; otherwise they'll be tuning to a false pitch. The hand position should be as open as possible in order to give a good clear sound and not change the pitch.

Tuba We should say that the warm-up does not have to start when you are in a room with your instrument. Carry the mouthpiece around with you during the day. It's great fun on a school bus . . .

Trumpet So we're creating air, lip and sound motion, and we're playing a basic pattern, a scale pattern in a nice relaxed way using lots of air and varying the dynamics. If you can only play loudly, try to get the vibration going in the mouthpiece and play softly down and up. Make like a fire siren, but slowly.

Trumpet In order to get the trumpet to sound properly, a good sound on the mouthpiece is necessary. Then the sound on the instrument will also be clear. So train your ear in pitch and try to get the best tone that you can. We're back to Tone and Tuning!

Tuba So far, I haven't heard anything that isn't similar. Maybe we need some different technique for the Tuba. We should stress that the Tuba player should *not* try to keep up with the players of smaller instruments insofar as breath phrases. He shouldn't try to make a long phrase. That's why I've given him twice as many breath marks in the book. As soon as you are out of air, take a breath. There is no award for duration. It is important to take a deep breath in and *get rid of it*. A nice big buzz. As soon as you are out of air, even for two quarter notes, take another breath.

Trombone But, that's true, in proportion for all the other brass players. You need air to make a really rich vibrant sound. What happens is that so many students starve for air, close off, and make the sound smaller. And there goes the Tone!

Trumpet But the section on breathing follows. Let's show another mouthpiece exercise which in a way sums up the others. Using your mouthpiece, start on a Concert Bb (c on a trumpet, f on a French Horn), play up a fifth (Trumpet: c d e f g f e d c). Then move up one note and repeat the exercise. Keep moving the bottom note up one note until you are at your fifth note in your beginning scale. Then, you have enough notes to play a whole octave – plus one note – on your mouthpiece. Do this in eighth notes when you can, with definite pitches, recognizable as a scale.

Trumpet So what we're saying is: Use your instrument to find beginning pitch, then warm up on your mouthpiece, using lots of air, gradually increasing your range, and playing definite pitches.

Horn And a little tip: get your whole group to play the piece you're working on *just on the mouthpiece*. Make the pitches true. You eliminate many instrumental problems and can concentrate on Tone and Tuning.

Trombone If you have a rhythmic problem, work it out on your mouthpiece, individually or as a group. We do it all the time.

Tuba Buzz the mouthpiece and play two or three or more bars just on the mouthpiece, and then back on the horn. You'll immediately hear a change in the sound; it will be richer and fuller. *Sing* your parts with the group to help in tuning; then back to the horn. Keep moving from mouthpiece, singing, and to the horn. The pitch, everything, is established right there, right at the mouthpiece. The instrument simply reflects the sound we're making. It amplifies it. The embouchure (your whole face) with your mouthpiece, and your ear – that's the important thing.

Breathing

It is very important that the student sit away from the back of the chair. SIT UP, NOT SIT DOWN! You should be sitting straight, but not rigidly straight. Lean forward just a little bit, take a deep breath and then, very easily, blow it out through your mouthpiece.

You should think that you are being held up by a hair from the top of your head – an imaginary hand is holding you up as you sit lightly on that chair, nice and erect.

We breathe in – a total breath. Not only is the chest expanding, the lungs filling up with wind, there may even be expansion and movement on the sides and back. Now breathe in and out slowly with the other members of the group, listening to them, and breathing together. 'The group that breathes together, plays together!' So now we have everyone breathing together, expanding and supporting. With your eyes closed, you should be able to hear and sense the other members of the group who are about to play a note, so that the attack is together with the air support together. Breathe in through the sides of your mouth and blow through the mouthpiece.

Think of the air column – not as the beam from a flashlight broadening drastically as it lengthens, but as a laser beam – focused, firm and alive. Keep your shoulders down, expand with the air coming in. The diaphragm drops, the ribs expand out, and the air is then supported and expelled as if your chest is a giant bellows.

If you are in doubt as to the muscles to be used for breathing, watch your dog or cat while it is sleeping. Expansion in the lower chest cavity is obvious. We've never seen a dog raise his shoulders when taking in air! So don't you. It only decreases the air capacity, tightens the throat muscles, and allows no support for the air. Besides, it looks funny!

Tonguing

Simply: "The tip of the Tongue to the Top" say 10 times.

Tonguing is articulation of notes, defining the beginning and attack. With rare exceptions (#4, #12, #13), the tonguing should be clean but smooth (legato). After saying the line above, follow your tongue to the place on the hard palate above the front teeth. Use that spot and say "Ta". This basic tonguing will suffice, and give a clear presentation.

The simple but important exercise of practicing "ta, ta, ta," can be accomplished when riding on a bus, sitting in a bathroom, or reading a book. Concentrate on only the TIP of your tongue contacting the palate. When rehearsing with your mouthpiece, make sure your tongue stays in its place, and does NOT move down between your teeth. You're on your way to clean, bright articulation!

Scales

Always practise the Scale of your piece playing the scale as musically as you can, producing your best TONE. Variations of Rhythm, Volume, and Breathing will help.

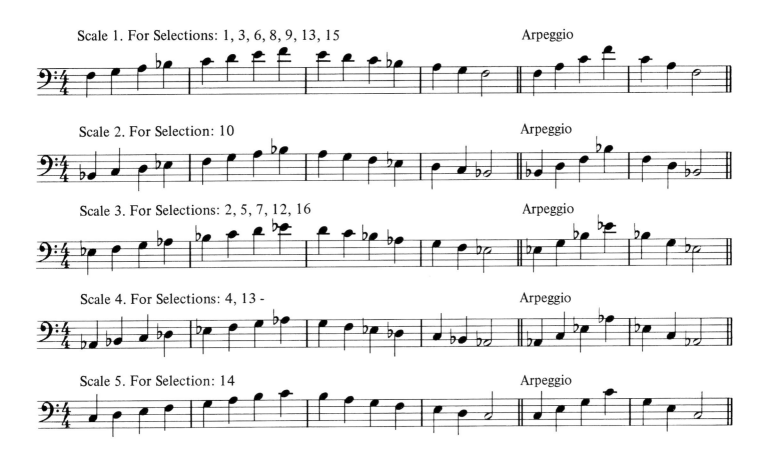

Hosanna

PALESTRINA

Scale: 1.

Palestrina was born near Rome, Italy about 1525. He began his musical training as a choirboy at the age of seven. Soon, he was recognized for his talent and was sent to a choir school in Rome. At the age of nineteen, he was appointed organist and choirmaster at the Cathedral in his home town. From then, until he died in 1594, he wrote Church music, attempting at a smoothness and beauty of sound rather than forceful expression.

Hosanna is a very simple example of his music. Notice the different styles between the opening and bar 16. The final six bars gives you an early introduction to 'imitation' — a melody repeated at different intervals in the different voices. We will see more of this in the next three selections, culminating in fugal imitation by Bach. Try to play *Hosanna* as smoothly as you can, tuning constantly.

This is an excellent test for Tone and Tuning. At times, you are an 'inner' part; you should listen to the parts around you for tuning. At other times (first 4 notes of phrase 1 & 2) you double the Tuba one octave higher and must tune the octave exactly with the Tuba. The phrases marked are probably too long for one breath. Otherwise, you'll close off and kill the rich vibrant sound you need. So 'sneak' breaths without anyone else knowing and without destroying the longer phrase.

The Canadian Brass

Non Nobis Domine

BYRD

Scale: 3.

William Byrd was born in England in 1543 and lived 80 years, composing music for the Church. Queen Elizabeth I was the ruler during most of his working life; Champlain explored America before Byrd died. He survived two Church 'reformations' and was not persecuted because his music was so valued. He was considered by many as the greatest composer of the 'Elizabethan' period. He wrote for choirs and keyboard instruments.

Non Nobis Domine is a famous 'Canon', in three parts with the melody unchanged from the unison, the fifth, and the octave. The word 'canon' means 'rule' and is a very strict imitation of the first voice. As such, you must play this piece with the same phrasing and smoothness in all three parts. If you wish to repeat (go *around* again) then stop at the asterisk (*) and go immediately to your first note, ignoring the preceding rest(s). Conclude at the double bar.

Since this is a CANON, our 'words of wisdom' are the same for every player. There must be unanimity in each phrase. That is, each phrase must sound the same at each entry. Play the piece together starting at your first *note* (though pitches will be different) and temporarily ignoring the opening rests. The smoothness, phrasing, dynamics must be equal in all instruments. Now, play as written, imitating each other faithfully.

The Canadian Brass

1. Hosanna!

Palestrina
(1525-1594)

2. Non Nobis Domine

(Canon)

Byrd
(1543-1623)

The Silver Swan

GIBBONS

Scale: 1.

Orlando Gibbons was born in England in 1583. He received his early musical training as a choirboy in King's College, Cambridge. He was considered a great choral and keyboard composer of the late Elizabethan period. He died in 1625 while he was organist of Westminster Abbey.

The Silver Swan is a classic and well-known example of his madrigals. Imitation was common in the contrapuntal writing of this time, and Gibbons was the master. Throughout the selection, there is imitation in all five voices, but it is not obvious. We have 'graphed' the parts below. Find your own part and follow it closely in your music. Colour your own line; then look for similar shaped phrases in the other four parts. You will find at least ten! When you perform this piece, be aware of the imitation.

The musical construction of this piece dictates the phrases as marked. However, the phrases are too long for proper breathing and free-flowing air. You will have to determine where to breathe without noticeably cutting up the musical sentence. (See P. 2, para. 5). But don't starve the air! Note pick-up to '8'. You and the 2nd Tpt are in a duet; then you pass the ball to F.H. Make sure that each of you play in the same style — smooth, with full tone. (Don't rush the dotted quarter).

The Canadian Brass

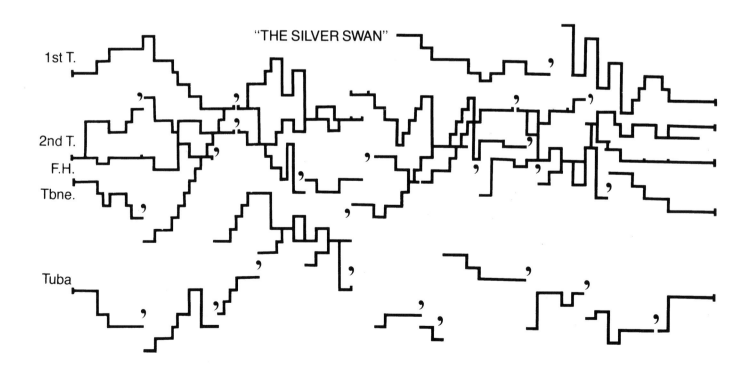

3. The Silver Swan

Gibbons
(1583-1625)

Exercise: 'Imitate' Each Other

THESE TWO EXERCISES SHOULD BE 'BUZZED' ON MOUTHPIECE. THEN, GO TO THE HORN.

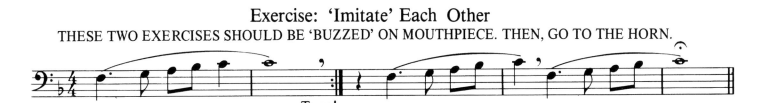

Tune!

Intrada
A fanfare
PEZEL

Scale: 4

Johann Pezel was born in Germany in 1639. He was a professional trumpet player himself, and wrote music for Brass Ensemble. The Fanfare is a good example of his characteristic brass writing and sophisticated use of rhythmic and chordal contrasts.

The opening pattern of three notes: ooO ooO gives you an excellent opportunity for tonguing exercise on scale 4. Keep the air column moving, with the tongue articulating the note as neatly as possible. Bar 3 & 4 need the tongue to move twice as quickly. Practice up to speed in your mouthpiece first. Crisp togetherness, with contrasting dynamics will make this Fanfare bright, lively and interesting.

The Canadian Brass

Fugue in E♭
BACH

Scale: 3.

Johann Sebastian Bach was born in Germany in 1685. His work represents the culmination in music up to his death in 1750. The imitation and canon that we have seen so far, all led to the 'Fugue'. The word 'Fugue' in French means 'flight'. This suggests that the opening part presents the melody (subject) then 'flies' before the following voices as they present the subject. Counterpoint, the interweaving of melodies, is the basis of all imitation, and ultimately, the fugue. Now, if you want to really understand what we have said, learn this simple, undeveloped fugue. Why not start with all players playing the first two bars of their own part at the same time, forgetting preceding rests. Now, you have the subject (melody). Then, learn the last 7 bars together. Now, start at the pick-up to bar 13. When all is in place, begin at the beginning, and put all the pieces together. Whenever you have the subject, you become the dominant part, and the other players support you; otherwise, you support the subject presented by the others. The climax of the piece is the Tuba entry leading to the conclusion of the Fugue. (A good example of a more complex Fugue is to be found on our records: *Fugue in G minor* (Little) by Bach. See if we keep the subject in mind and in front of you always.) Have fun!

Again, imitation between all parts is essential in the performance of any fugue. Your phrases should show a nice curve to the dynamic shape, support for the upper notes of the phrase, and a bright tone. A breath before the last note, if taken by everyone, will give a slight silent space before the final chord and make the cadence stronger and more emphatic. This is the simplest shortest Bach fugue that I know, but is a good introduction to one of my favourite forms and composers.

The Canadian Brass

4. Intrada-A Fanfare

Pezel
(1639-1694)

5. Fugue in E♭

Bach
(1685-1750)

'Air' from Water Music

HANDEL

Scale: 1.

George Friedrich Handel was also German, born in 1685 like Bach, but spent most of his musical life in England as the court musician for George III (who himself was German!). Handel and Bach are a curious pair: Bach reflected the past and brought it to the peak; Handel knew the past, used it, but projected more into the future. He also lived nine years longer, travelled much more, and made much more money.

The *'Air'* is a simple, melodic movement from a Suite that Handel composed for the King of England. It was to provide nice background music as the King sailed down the Thames River through London in 1717. You will notice the immediate difference from #1 − 5 in this book. Handel's music is more dominant in the top and bottom part, rather than equally voiced. The melody is very important. Try to play the dotted notes longer and the following notes shorter than you think they should be. Mathematically, they must be 3:1 ratio. This selection will provide you and your audience with a great deal of satisfaction, representing as it does Handel at his finest.

Learning our math − Lesson 1

In everyday activities, we make comparisons.
Dodgers beat the Yankees 3 runs to 1.
This can be written as a ratio − 3:1.
We can show this by looking at a Baseball Scorecard.

Inning:	1	2	3	4	5	6	7	8	9
Dodgers			X			X		X	
Yankees					X				

If we assemble the marked squares, we have a picture of our ratio.

$\boxed{1}\boxed{2}\boxed{3}$
$\boxed{1}$

or, better − $\boxed{1}\boxed{2}\boxed{3}$: $\boxed{1}$

In music, notes have ratios.

$$\text{♩.} : \text{♩} = (\text{♩} + \text{♩} + \text{♩} : \text{♩}) \qquad = 3:1$$

or

$$\text{♪.} : \text{♪} = (\text{♪} + \text{♪} + \text{♪} : \text{♪}) \qquad = 3:1$$

or, it could be written ♪♪ =3:1

The total of our ratio 3:1 is 4.

So we can say that the ♪. is 3/4, and the ♪ is 1/4.

Count to 4 and keep repeating − 1 2 3 4, 1 2 3 4, etc.
Now, clap the ratio of 1 2 3 4, 1 2 3 4, 1 2 3 4, etc.

You now have the musical time ratio of ♪♪

So − □□□ : □ =3:1
   or 1 2 3 : 1 =3:1
   or ♪. : ♪ =3:1

In the *Air*, it is so important that every player present his ♪♪ in a true 3:1 ratio.

The Canadian Brass

---

6. 'Air' from Water Music

Handel
(1685-1759)

Ave Verum

MOZART

Scale: 3.

Wolfgang Amadeus Mozart was born in Austria in 1756, six years after the death of Bach. Music had progressed in many different directions since the culmination of Bach and the development of Handel. The selection presented here is not typical, on the surface, of Mozart, but in depth, is one of his simplest but finest creations using the limited resources of choir, rather than the extensive resources of the now-developed instrumental ensemble. Mozart was a child prodigy — that is, an extraordinary person who at the age of four composed the world's best known song: *Twinkle, Twinkle Little Star!*

'Ave Verum' was written very late in Mozart's life as he contemplated life following death. The work should be played with a sense of dignity, slowly, and with a full tone. This is a marvellous selection for a real concentration on tuning, tone and balance, the three real ingredients for good ensemble playing. We have included this example over all others of Mozart because of the sheer beauty of its line, harmony and shape. Most of Mozart's music seems much lighter, but all is very hard to perform in proper style. This selection plays into your hearts and flows with its own dignity. We think that you will like it.

The Canadian Brass

7. Ave Verum

Mozart
(1756-1791)

Ave Maria

RACHMANINOFF

Scale: 1.

Sergey Rachmaninoff was born in Russia in 1873. He was educated musically through the piano and later in life was also considered an excellent orchestral conductor. Even though he died in 1943, not many years ago, his music is considered as belonging to the nineteenth century. He met Tschaikovsky when he was fifteen years old, when Tschaikovsky was 48 and only 5 years from death.

Ave Maria (Hail, Mary, Mother of God) is one of the few well-known choral pieces by Rachmaninoff. It is a fascinating and very powerful statement of music, utilizing the techniques of the Romantic composers in building surely and carefully to an emotional climax, while still reflecting almost the classical period of choral writing.

Let's look at the composition in depth. It opens in a very clear but thin 'texture' — a duet of the two trumpet parts. They must sound as one but in thirds. The horn joins and complements the other two, adding also a tonal colour needed for a greater depth. The trombone enters on a descending passage and creates four-part harmony, which immediately disintegrates into moving thirds between horn and 2nd Tpt, while the Trombone and 1st Tpt, in octaves, start a new melody. Any climax is built on tension, and we are now past the opening lyrical phrases and into the body. Notice that the breathing and phrasing between the two components is quite different, starting at bar 15 and carrying on until the Tuba entry at bar 21. The strongest melody is presented by the Tuba, doubled by the French Horn, while the Trumpets and Trombone continue with the previous thought. Do you realize that this is characteristic of the counterpoint of the 16th and 17th century that was discussed in numbers 1-4 of this book? The *'Ave Maria'* comes to a tranquil conclusion with a simple almost puritanical chordal structure for the last four bars. What an interesting study of texture, counterpoint, and climaxes all within 28 bars and 1½ minutes! Try to sense the emotion.

Learning our math — Lesson 2

Theorem: Lines of equal slopes are parallel, and
Slopes of parallel lines are equal.

In the *Ave Maria,* we find two different and important uses of this theorem: 1) *Parallel motion in thirds:*

Examples: 1st & 2nd Tpts. Bar 1-4, 8, 21, 22, 25.
2nd Tpt & F.H. Bars 14-20, 24, Tbne & Tuba Bars 25-6

2) *Parallel motion in octaves:*

Examples: 1st Tpt & Tbne. Bars 15-23
F.H. & Tuba Bars 20-22

Rule The Lower Part must be equal, both tuned and 'married' to the top part. You must identify with the other part. The lower part must play louder and project more to be 'equal'.

8. Ave Maria

Rachmaninoff
(1873-1943)

By permission of Boosey & Hawkes (Canada) Ltd., Toronto

Cwm Rhondda

WELSH

Scale: 1.

Wales is a 'state' of Britain. The Britons were defeated by the English many centuries ago, and were pushed to the far West coast of the Island. There, they kept to many of their own traditions, language, and pace of life. A need for energy developed following the Industrial Revolution, and coal mines were opened in Wales. The local workers found solace in their long dangerous hours in the pits by singing and harmonizing Hymn tunes. *Cwm Rhondda* is the most famous of all these songs.

We are now half-way through our book, and it seems like a great place to "re-capitulate our exposition" — to re-state our objectives and develop your thinking further.

Tone: The 'sound' that we make must not be forgotten as we get into more complicated notes, fingerings or rhythms, or as our range becomes extended. A player with poor tone is a player not to be enjoyed by the audience.

Tuning: Again, as range is extended in the next few selections, tuning becomes more important. The support of the air column, the speed and intensity of the air column will support the tone, and allow you careful tuning.

Balance: The next few arrangements create balance problems which can be overcome with careful listening. *Cwm Rhondda* appears so simple, but is an excellent exercise in all three areas above.

Blend: We have purposely not mentioned Blend earlier. The counterpoint in the music called for a more characteristic sound of the individual instrument than the individual instrument 'blending' into the ensemble. But, when we are performing 'harmonic' music, chordal music, we want to create more of a Blend — five people with one sound rather than five separate sounds. This is achieved through listening, thinking together, and the attempt to make one sound out of four distinctly different instrumental sounds.

Rhythm: Further, you will find: *Bones,* and the first of *Three Newfoundland Folksongs.* Each has a driving forward, pulsating rhythm that must sound as one. Be careful with your *Timing* of notes and rests; try to think as one player, not as many individuals. Sense the motion.

Colour: Each instrument has its own colour, determined by the construction: a Trumpet and Trombone are two-thirds cylindrical, one-third conical; therefore the tone is more focused and brighter. The French Horn (with a different overtone series — ask your teacher) and the Tuba are more conical; therefore the tone is more mellow, more singing. The second of the *Three Newfoundland Folksongs* gives the French Horn a chance to emphasize its characteristics.

The *Farewell Anthem* demands from all a smooth singing quality, especially in the overlapping of parts. The accents in *Bones* are better suited to the focused sound of the Trumpets and Trombones, but all instruments must participate in the dynamic effect. Bring your own colour to your group, but do not let the individuality of your instrument or you conflict with the unity of the whole. The Finale *Three Newfoundland Folksongs* provides all of you with a challenge in each of the six areas above. Enjoy yourself!

9. Cwm Rhondda

Welsh

Carol of the Bells

UKRAINIAN

Scale: 2 (but related MINOR)

A peal of bells is heard, faintly, now getting closer, now fading away. The Tuba acts as the big and constant 'Bonger', while the other four voices take turns presenting the short subject /—/, /—/, /—/, /—/. Whenever you play that rhythm, present it exactly as your group has decided, so that it is constant. The other melodies support it, never dominating.

The Tbne. entry gives you an excellent chance to make the notes speak like a bell, with good clean beginning articulation. Watch bar 21-24. Second position is tight to first, not half-way between 1 & 4. Bar 25-28; try 'D' in fourth — more in tune and easier. Bar 33 to end; concentrate on 'bell' sound.

The Canadian Brass

El Yivneh Hagalil

ISRAEL

Scale: There is no tonic scale, as the music comes from a period long before tonality. Modes preceded tonic scales. The Mode of EL YIVNEH is: Me Fah Se Lah Te Lah
(Intervals in Step) $\frac{1}{2}$ 1 $\frac{1}{2}$ $\frac{1}{2}$ 1
Fah should feel very flat; *Se* should feel very sharp.

El Yivneh Hagalil (The Lord will build a new Galilee) is a work song of the fields. Notice the strong rhythm when all the instruments are put together. This is a cumulative song in that parts are added in each verse. Following the Tuba part in *Carol of the Bells,* it seems appropriate to draw your attention to the Tuba solo! Here is the construction:
Tuba; Tuba & Tbne; Tuba, Tbne & Horn; Tuba, Tbne, Horn & 2nd Tpt; Tuba, Tbne, Horn, Tpts.

Finally, the tuba has the limelight. So, now it is our turn to support. The tuba sets the tempo, the rhythm, the pitch and the pulse. It is up to the rest of us to decorate the tuba part with long notes using our best tone and concentrating on tuning. The tuning is very difficult because we are playing in fourths and fifths. When you get to measure 33, go full out right to the end. Watch the off-beat penultimate bar. Big crescendo right through the last bar will make this a great concert piece or encore.

The Canadian Brass

10. Carol of the Bells

Ukrainian

11. El Yivneh Hagalil

Israel

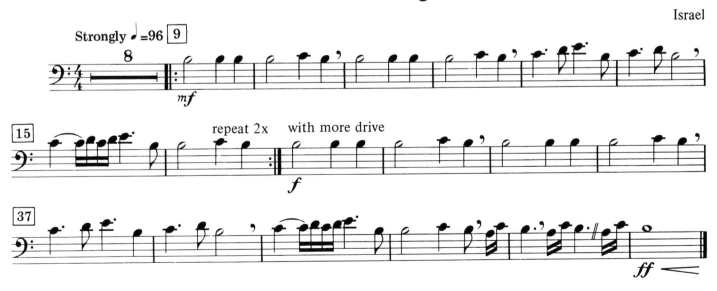

12. Bones

13. Three Newfoundland Folksongs

14. The Lord Bless You and Keep You
(Farewell Anthem)

Peter Lutkin
(1858-1931) U. S. A.

15. My Country, Tis of Thee/God Save the Queen

16. O Canada!

Lavallée

A 'note' on performance

Music is an 'outward and visible sound of an inward and spiritual grace'. It's a joy for the individual though requiring much private practice. When brought to a group i.e. Brass Quintet, it is to be shared with the other players, just as they share with the individual. Careful attention to all detail will result in a unity of sound and thought within a social interaction.

Our music can now be shared with others – an audience. This is the true joy of performance. But certain new ideas must be kept in mind.

Programming: Choose numbers from this book or your repertoire which reflect different styles, different keys, different moods and dynamics.

Example A:	Hosanna	Palestrina
Easy	Intrada	Pezel
	Cwm Rhondda	Welsh
	My Country/God Save the Queen	
Example B:	The Silver Swan	Gibbons
Medium	Fugue in E^b	Bach
	El Yivneh Hagalil	Israeli
	Three Newfoundland Folksongs	Canadian
Example C:	Air (from Water Music)	Handel
Difficult	Carol of the Bells (anytime)	Ukrainian
	Ave Maria	Rachmaninoff
	Bones	Spiritual

Don't be afraid of using *O Canada*. Though it is the Anthem of Canada, it is also a good melody and will complement any programme.

Or, mix Easy, Medium and Difficult pieces to suit yourself and your audience. The listeners are not present to hear technical achievement; they want a pleasant selection of music. The good performer never allows the audience to notice technical difficulties, so choose music well within the group's capabilities.

The performance begins as you enter and finishes when you leave. Be aware of all visual details and keep distraction to a minimum.

We have constantly stressed the enjoyment of the Brass medium and the music. Try to convey this to your audience. It is infectious, and will bring real pleasure to them. Above all, enjoy yourself!

See you in the Concert Hall!

The Canadian Brass